모든 벽은 문이다

모든 벽은 문이다

박헌영 조형시집
2025

이든북

책머리에

과거로 돌아갈 수 있다면 돌아갈 것인가? 현대문명을 부정적으로 보는 것만은 아니다. 인간의 조건에서 문명은 정신문화와 함께 생명과도 같다. 그 생명의 진화와 퇴화, 즉 돌아오고 상승하는 이중나선 같은 궤적을 조형시로 표현했다. 희망을 촉매로.

제1부는 조형시집 『나의 거울』 중 개작한 작품들이고 제2부는 재수록한 작품들이다.

아들에게 고맙다.

2025년 5월
샘머리정자에서
박헌영

Preface

If you could go back to the past, would you go back? It is not that I only see modern civilization negatively. In the human condition, civilization is like life along with spiritual culture. the evolution and degeneration of that life, that is, the trajectory like a double helix that returns and rises, is expressed in a form- poem(Johyeongshi). hope as a catalyst.

Part 1 consists of revised works from the form-poem collection 〈My Mirror〉, and part 2 consists of re-incorporated works.

Thank you son.

May 2025

At Sammeori pavilion

Park Hun-young

| 차례 |

책머리에 ····················· 04

제1부 나의 거울

나의 거울 ····················· 13
시간은 안녕하신가 ····················· 15
화석연료가 다할 무렵 ····················· 17
아버지 ····················· 19
자화상 ····················· 21
여선생 ····················· 23

제2부 창인가 TV인가

창인가 TV인가	29
마음의 진화	31
무거운 눈물	33
불멸의 쓰레기	35
APT	37
너무 큰 해바라기	39
재두루미	41
희망 혹은 삶에 대하여	43
베 짜는 밤	45

제3부 문

문 ····················· 49
당산나무 ····················· 51
나무부처 ····················· 53
나무예수 ····················· 55
뿔 ····················· 57
꼬꼬마 자전거 ····················· 59
책장 ····················· 61
청룡언월도 ····················· 63
우유 한 팩 ····················· 65
죽은 별 ····················· 67
꽃눈에게 ····················· 69
돌 하나 ····················· 71
아이들 함께 ····················· 73
돌의 정원-매화 ····················· 75

돌의 정원-난초 ·················· 77
돌의 정원-국화 ·················· 79
돌의 정원-대나무 ················ 81
희망의 힘으로.2 ················· 83
희망의 힘으로.3 ················· 85
희망의 힘으로.8 ················· 87
희망의 힘으로.9 ················· 89
희망의 힘으로.10 ················ 91
초롱이탑.2 ······················ 93
연리지連理枝 ····················· 95
눈물 위 ·························· 97
병풍 ····························· 99
소실점에서 ·················· 101

 제1부

나의 거울

나의 거울 (My mirror)
4×77×139cm
자개, 회로기판, 구리철사 (circuit board, mother-of-pearl, copper wire)
2022

나의 거울

새가 새를 볼 수 있게
나무가 나무를 볼 수 있게
별이 별을 볼 수 있게
내가 나를 볼 수 있게
도시여, 거울을 돌려다오.

My mirror

So that the bird can see the bird

So that the tree can see the tree

So that the stars can see the stars

So that I can see myself

City, give back the mirror.

시간은 안녕하신가 (How's the time)
103×207.5×35.5cm
회로기판, 구리철사, 벽시계, 자개, 전선
(circuit board, copper wire, wall clock, mother-of-pearl, wire)
2024

시간은 안녕하신가

100년 후의 서울에 바퀴가 굴러간다.
둥근 하늘이 일그러진다.

How's the time

The wheels roll in Seoul 100 years later.
The round sky is distorted.

화석연료가 다할 무렵 (When Fossil Fuels End)
7×35×35cm
구리철사, 회로기판, 알루미늄 캔, 알루미늄 호일
(copper wire, circuit board, aluminum can, aluminum foil)
2025

화석연료가 다할 무렵

수상도시인가.
노아의 방주인가.

When Fossil Fuels End

Is it a water city?
Is it Noah's Ark?

아버지 (Father)
28×32×63cm
구리철사, 구리판, 전선, 목재 (copper wire, copper plate, wire, wood)
2024

아버지

바람결 종잇장 같은 삶에
지층은 켜켜이 두터웠다.

병든 아내
삶을 모르는 아들 셋.

'먹는 것에 타락하지 마라.'
당신 말씀은 대들보였다.

예순세 살에 떠올라 가버린
짐자전거 한 생.

Father

In a life like a piece of paper in the wind,
The layers were thick.

A sick wife.
Three sons who don't know life.

'Don't be corrupted by eating.'
Your words were the main beam.

Came to mind and go away at the age of sixty-three,
A life of a luggage bike.

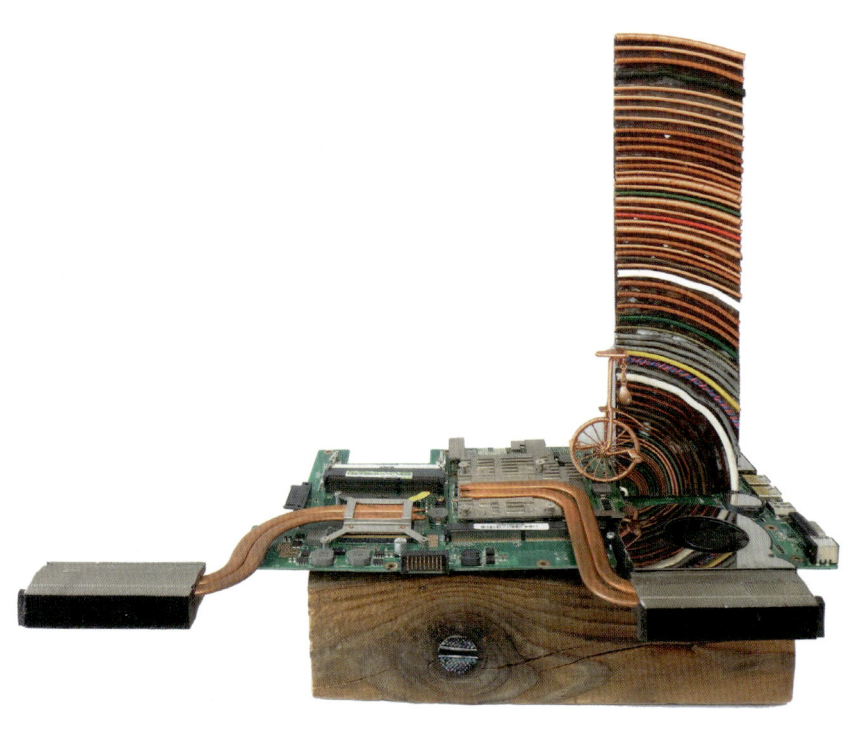

자화상 (Self-portrait)
19×38×35cm
구리철사, 회로기판, 자개, 전선 (copper wire, circuit board, mother-of-pearl, wire)
2023

자화상

나의 새는 눈멀지 않았다.
어린 날 상처는 DNA보다 깊어
겨울 나이테로 겹겹 날 가두었지만
술 한잔 담배 한 모금 있어도 없어도
가로등 필라멘트는 항상 새였다.
한쪽 날개는 불구였으나 새였다.
가로등 가시 불빛에 다시
눈물 어린다.

Self-portrait

My bird was not blind.

The wounds of my childhood were deeper than DNA

The winter tree rings trapped me in layers,

But whether I had a drink or a puff of cigarette,

The streetlight filament was always a bird.

Even though one wing was crippled, it was a bird.

The streetlight thorn light brought tears

To my eyes again.

여선생 (female teacher)
13×14×60cm
회로기판, 구리철사, 모래 (circuit board, copper wire, sand)
2022

여선생

제대한 그해 유성에서
조그만 다리공사 현장으로
막일을 다녔었지
다릿발이 서고 상판이 놓여갈 즈음
거푸집 짓는 김목수는 김목수대로
발동기로 괸물 퍼내는 최기사는 최기사대로
똑같은 기다림과 기쁨이 있었음을
서로들 말없이 알게 되었지
둑길 옆 초등학교로 갓 발령난 그녀가
흙가마니로 임시 만든 징검다리를
조심스레 건너갈 때면
우린 서로의 맑은 속심을 나누며
손발에 환히 차오르는 힘을 느꼈지
그녀의 출근길이 가슴을 짚어 오면
행여 그 눈빛 마주칠세라
햇살 부서지는 제비꽃에 눈 두었고
멀리서부터 둑길 휘어 오는
그녀의 퇴근길 늦은 오후가 되면
계룡산 기슭의 부우연 바람꽃으로
다시 또 눈길 돌리곤 했던 그 봄,
준공날이 오기 며칠 전
우리의 어깨 같은 다리 위로

그녀의 가느란 다리가 건너는 걸 못 보고
모두들 다음 현장으로 떠나가야 했었지
황사바람 부는 도치마을 들길에서
제비꽃을 바라보다 문득 떠오른 그 때,
빚더미로 병든 어머니를 구완하며
두 동생의 학비를 돕던 그 현장,
김목수가 그립고 최기사가 그리고
여선생을 그리워하던 내가 그립다
오늘 가만히 머리 들어
맑은 날 올랐을 적 계룡산이 보였던
저 미륵산 기슭의 바람꽃으로
마음 속 하얀 옛 다리를 놓는다
어디선가 아이들의 눈빛 기르는 그녀를
내 이제는 만나리라며.

female teacher

Yuseong the year I was discharged
To a small bridge construction site I had a bad jobAs the bridge was erected and the top was laid,
Carpenter Kim who was building the formwork
And engineer Choi who was shoveling the water with a motor
We all silently realized
That there was the same waiting and joy.
When she, who had just been assigned to the elementary school

Next to the embankment,
Carefully crossed the temporary stepping stones
We shared our clear thoughts with each other
And felt the strength rising in our hands and feet.
When her way to work touches my heart
In fear of our eyes meeting,
I kept my eyes on the violet flowers shining in the sunlight,
In the spring, when her commute home
From work came late in the afternoon,
I would turn my gaze again to the windflowers
To the foot of Mt. Gyeryong.A few days before the completion date,
We couldn't see her slender legs
Crossing over our shoulder-like bridges
Everyone had to leave for the next construction site.
On the field road of Dochi Village
Where the yellow sand wind blows
When I was looking at the violets,
It suddenly occurred to me.
Helping my mother who was sick due to debt
I helped my two younger siblings pay their tuition,
The construction site where
I miss carpenter Kim, engineer Choi
And I miss myself who missed the female teacher.
Quietly lift my head today
Mt. Mireuk, where I could see Mt. Gyeryong
When I climbed it on a clear day
To the wind flower at the foot of Mt. Mireuk
Building a white old bridge in my heart.
Somewhere who raises the eyes of children
I will meet her.

제2부

창인가 TV인가

창인가 TV인가 (Window or TV)
4×62×62cm
구리철사, 회로기판, 플라스틱 (copper wire, circuit board, plastic)
2020

창인가 TV인가

사면 벽에 든 영혼이여,
TV를 숨 쉬는가
하늘을 숨 쉬는가.
999개의 채널이 돌아가고
새는 날아가네.

Window or TV

Soul in the four walls,

Breathing TV

Breathing the sky.

999 channels are spinning

Birds are flying.

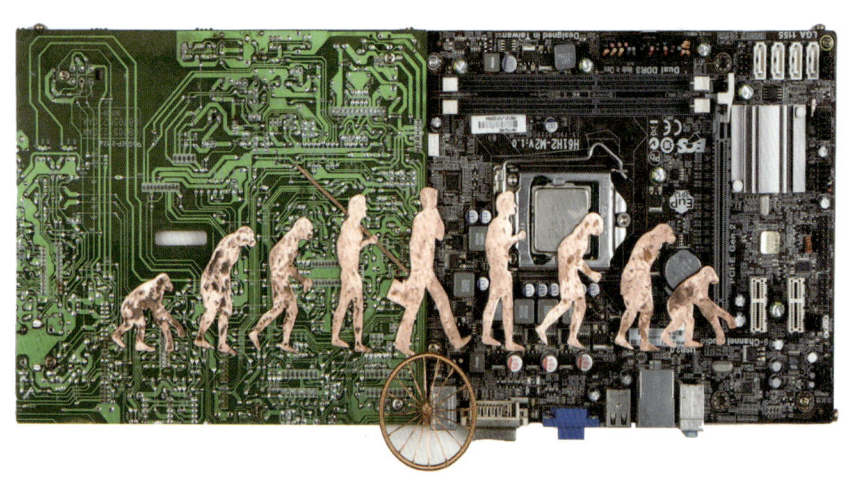

마음의 진화 (Evolution of the mind)
4×53×31cm
구리철사, 회로기판, 구리판, 플라스틱 (copper wire, circuit board, copper plate, plastic)
2020

마음의 진화

진화와 퇴화는 공존한다.
우리는 무엇이 진화하는가.
무엇이 퇴화하는가.

태극인가.
이중나선인가.

Evolution of the mind

Evolution and degeneration coexist.
What are we evolving?
What are we degenerating?

Is it a Taegeuk?
Is it a double helix?.

무거운 눈물 (Heavy Tears)
24×37.5×10cm
구리철사, 회로기판, 구리판 (copper wire, circuit board, copper plate)
2020

무거운 눈물

문명의 뒤안길을 헤매이는
별들의 눈물방울,
납이 된.

Heavy Tears

Teardrops of stars wandering

The back streets of civilization,

Became lead.

불멸의 쓰레기 (Immortal Trash)
26×36×6.5cm
구리철사, 회로기판, 플라스틱, 나사 (coper wire, circuit boards, plastic, screws)
2020

불멸의 쓰레기

대지가 만든 산.
인간이 만든
쓰레기 피라미드.

Immortal Trash

Mountains made by the Earth.
Pyramids of Man-made Trash.

APT (APT)
19×26×40cm
구리철사, 회로기판, 알루미늄 (copper wire, circuit board, aluminum)
2020

APT

아파트 60억 원,
60억 원짜리 감옥에 산다.

APT

Apartment worth 6 billion won,
Living in a 6 billion won prison.

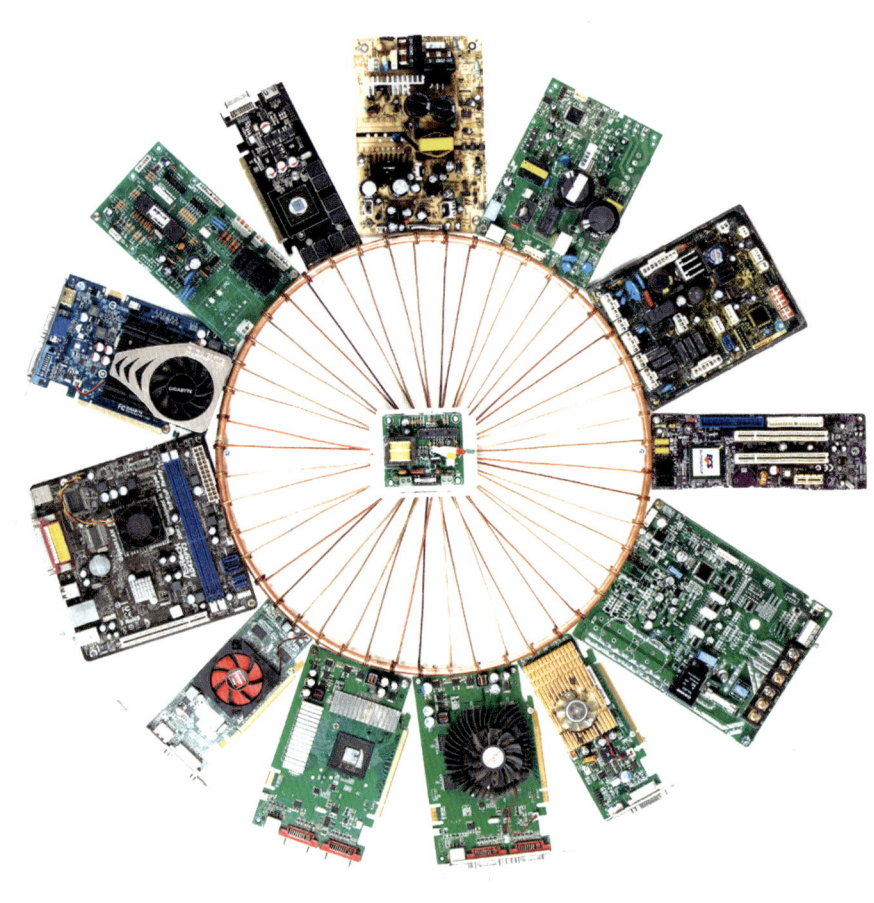

너무 큰 해바라기 (Too Big Sunflower)
8×76×90,5cm
회로기판, 구리철사 (circuit board, copper wire)
2020

너무 큰 해바라기

옛 희망은 희망을 비껴갔나.
희망을 지나쳤나.

Too Big Sunflower

Did the old hopes move aside the hope?

Did they passed hope?

재두루미 (white-naped crane)
24.5×24.5×8.5cm
회로기판, 구리철사, 구리판, 화강암 가루
(circuit board, copper wire, copper plate, granite powder)
2021

재두루미

때 묻은 날개가 아니면
하늘을 날아보았다고 말하지 말라.

white-naped crane

Unless it's a dirty wing
Don't say you flew in the sky.

희망 혹은 삶에 대하여(About hope or life)
126.5×74×25cm
구리철사, 회로기판(copper wire, circuit board)
2020

희망 혹은 삶에 대하여

넘어지지 않는 자
무너지지 않는 자 어디 있느냐.
쓰러진 길이 당신에게
왕관을 씌운다.

About hope or life

Who doesn't stumble?
The path you have fallen down
Crowns you.

베 짜는 밤 (Weaving Cotton fabric At night)
5×100×59cm
회로기판, 구리철사, 베틀목, 베, 무명실, 구리판
(Circuit board, copper wire, loom, cotton, cotton thread, copper plate)
2020

베 짜는 밤

달가닥 달가닥
달밤 외할머니가 무명베를 짠다.
자정 너머 새벽으로 간다.

씨줄은 문명인가.
날줄은 문화인가.
씨줄은 인간인가.
날줄은 자연인가.

인간이여,
네 죽음은
문명을 갖고 가지 못한다.

문화에 문명이 어울고
자연에 인간이 어울고.

달가닥 달가닥
오늘 밤도 외할머니는
위선 경선처럼
무늬를 짠다.

Weaving Cotton fabric At night

Dalgadak dalgadak
On a moonlit night,
My maternal grandmother weaves cotton fabric.
It goes past midnight and into dawn.

Is the weft civilization?
Is the warp culture?
Is the weft human?
Is the warp nature?

Human,
Your death
Cannot take civilization with you.

Civilization harmonizes with culture,
And humans harmonize with nature.

Dalgadak dalgadak
Tonight, too,
My maternal grandmother weaves patterns
Like latitude and longitude.

 제3부

문

문 (Door)
8×138×185cm
회로기판, 자개, 구리철사 (circuit board, mother-of-pearl, copper wire)
2023

문

모든 벽은 문이다.
벽 전체는 문이다.
완전히 닫힌 문은 결코 없다.
열지 못했을 뿐.

과거는 미래의 문,
운명은 나의 문이다.

우리는 모두가 모두의 벽이다.
모두가 모두의 문이다.

Door

Every wall is a door.
The whole wall is a door.
There is never a door that is completely closed.
I just couldn't open it.

The past is the door to the future,
Destiny is my door.

We are everyone's wall.
Everyone is everyone's door.

당산나무 (Dangsan tree)
6×207×103cm
구리철사, 회로기판, 자개, 느티나무 껍질
(copper wire, circuit board, mother-of-pearl, zelkova bark)
2023

당산나무

죽은 나무 느티나무에 문을 단다.
죽지 않는 뿌리가 걸어나온다.

Dangsan tree

Hang the door on a dead tree zelkova tree.
The roots that don't die come out.

나무부처 (A wooden Buddha)
44×139×123cm
향나무 가지, 구슬, 회로기판, 구리철사
(juniper branch, beads, circuit boards, copper wire)
2023

나무부처

천수천안千手千眼.

눈 있는 자 마음 있는 자, 보라.
저 나무부처!

A wooden Buddha

A thousand hands and a thousand trees千手千眼.

Those with eyes, those with hearts, look.
That wooden Buddha!

나무예수 (Wooden Jesus)
6×31×46cm
구리철사, 회로기판, 자개, 알루미늄 호일
(copper wire, circuit board, mother-of-pearl, aluminum foil)
2022

나무예수

나무가 자라서 나무 예수가 되어
성당유치원 졸업식장에서 나무 눈을 감고 있다.

…안녕히 계셔요. 예수님
　우리 예수님 안녕 안녕

골 깊은 갈비뼈,
갈비뼈에 나이테가 한 줄 더 그려진다.

나무들이 나무를 졸업하는 소란 위에서
안 보이는 당신 몸을 홀로 보고 있다.

　　　　Wooden Jesus

　　　　The tree grew and became a wooden Jesus,
　　　　And closed his tree eyes,
　　　　At the graduation ceremony of the cathedral kindergarten.

　　　　Goodbye. Jesus Our Jesus
　　　　goodbye, goodbye

　　　　Deep ribs,
　　　　Another line is drawn from the ribs.

　　　　Above the noise of trees graduating from trees
　　　　You are looking at your invisible body alone.

뿔 (Horn)
120×60.5×24.5cm
회로기판, 자개, 나무뿌리, 구리철사
(circuit board, mother-of-pearl, tree root, copper wire)
2023

뿔

나무는 죽었는가.
잎은 떨어져 바람을 덮고
줄기는 쓰러져 길을 파묻는가.
눈물은 이윽고
단단한 관솔이 된다.
뿌리는 뼈,
썩을 수 없는 자의 뼈,
생의 모든 밤으로 솟구치는
뿔이여.
횃불이여.

Horn

Is the tree dead?
The leaves fall off and cover the wind
Does the stem fall and bury the way.
Tears will come out soon
It becomes a pine knots.
Root is bones,
The bones of the rotless,
Soaring into every night of one's life
It's a horn.
It's a torchlight.

꼬꼬마 자전거 (Very small bike)
5×18×16.5cm
구리철사, 회로기판 (copper wire, circuit board)
2023

꼬꼬마 자전거

세상에서 제일 큰 영혼이 타는 자전거.

Very small bike

The bike ridden by the biggest soul in the world.

책장 (Bookshelf)
28.5×120.5×201.5cm
목재 책장, 회로기판, 달항아리, 자개판, 구리철사 (wooden bookshelf, circuit board, moon jar, mother-of-pearl plate, copper wire)
2025

책장

무엇을 읽는가.
뇌는 무엇을 사는가.
교감신경은 어디에 연결되었는가.
부교감신경은 어떻게 깔려 있는가.
심장은 왜 뛰는가.
왜 읽는가.

Bookshelf

What do you read?

What does the brain live?

Where are the sympathetic nerves connected?

How are the parasympathetic nerves laid out?

Why does the heart beat?

Why do you read?

청룡언월도 (chuengryolungunwoldo)
31.5×33.5×21.5cm
회로기판, 구리철사 (circuit board, copper wire)
2023

청룡언월도

명검은 함부로 휘두르지 않는다.
악을 치면서 빛의 문을 열며.

chuengryolungunwoldo

A great sword is not wielded carelessly.
Striking evil, opening the door of light.

우유 한 팩 (A pack of milk)
4×5.5×11.5cm
우유팩, 회로기판, 빨대, 구리철사 (milk pack, circuit board, straw, copper wire)
2023

우유 한 팩

자식은 너인가?
너인가?

자식 없는 모유母乳가
각角을 채운다.

A pack of milk

Is your child you?

Is it you?

The mother's milk without children

Fills an angle.

죽은 별 (Dead star)
40×34.5×2.5cm
회로기판, 알루미늄 호일, 구리철사 (circuit board, aluminum foil, copper wire)
2023

죽은 별

밤하늘에 별은 죽었다.
죽어서도 빛난다.
본래 네 것이 아니었기에.

Dead star

The stars died in the night sky.
Even if die, shine.
Because it's not originally yours.

꽃눈에게 (To the flower buds)
21×30.5×5.5cm
회로기판, 구리철사, 나뭇가지, 스티로폼, 종이
(circuit board, copper wire, branches, styrofoam, paper)
2023

꽃눈에게

모든 겨울은
꽃샘추위다.
나목을 보면
3월 1일 백일홍나무를 보면
더더욱.

To the flower buds

Every winter is

Spring cold.

Look at bare tree

On March 1st,

Look at the crimson tree

Even more.

돌 하나 (A stone)
30.5×19.5×5cm
회로기판, 구리철사, 돌 (circuit board, copper wire, ston)
2024

돌 하나

길 가다 돌 하나 집어들었다.
어느 아이인지 크레용으로 무지개를 그려넣었다.
돌 속에 숨긴 내 수많은 손금의 길들,
눈발은 비가 되고
비는 눈물이 되고,
어느덧 하류에 다다라
비뚤어졌지만 나름 둥근 돌이 되었다.
손금에 집어들었다.
나는 인생을 놓지 않았다.
살아 있는 자는 모두 그렇다.
아이들의 놀이에서
내 눈물에 어린 무지개를
놓칠 수는 없었다.

A stone

I picked up a stone on the road.
Some kid drew a rainbow with a crayon.
The countless paths of my palms hidden in the stone,
Snowfall becomes rain
And rain becomes tears,
And before I knew it, it reached the downstream,
And became a crooked but round stone.
I picked it up in my palm.
I didn't give up on life.
All living beings are like that.
In the children's play,
I couldn't miss the rainbow in my tears.

아이들과 함께 (With children)
45×45×1.5cm
회로기판, 구리철사, 구리판, 알루미늄 호일
(circuit board, copper wire, copper plate, aluminum foil)
2024

아이들 함께

샘머리아파트 팔각정자는
회로기판 위에 떠 있는 섬.
봄에도 봄
소낙비에도 봄
낙엽에도 봄
흰눈에도 봄,
봄섬.

With children

The octagonal pavilion of Sammeori Apartment is
An island floating on a circuit board.
Spring too
Spring even in the rain
Spring in the fall of leaves
Spring even in white snow,
Spring Island.

돌의 정원-매화 (A garden of stones- plum blossom)
/ 35×60×1cm
회로기판, 알루미늄 호일, 구리철사 (circuit board, aluminum foil, copper wire)
2023

돌의 정원
- 매화

저 돌,
흙이 되어
마들가리 끝에서
설매화
피우리라.

A garden of stones
- plum blossom

That stone,
Become dirt
At the end Madegari
Snow plum blossom
Will bloom.

돌의 정원-난초 (A garden of stones-orchid)
3×46×33.5cm
회로기판, 구리철사, 알루미늄 호일, 알루미늄 캔
(circuit board, copper wire, aluminum foil, aluminum can)
2023

돌의 정원
- 난초

난을 25년이나 키우면서도
정작 난시蘭詩를 못 쓰고 있네.
난을 키웠을 뿐
난심蘭心을 키우지 못했네.
돌의 정원이네.

A garden of stones
- orchid

I raised orchid for 25 years
I can't really write an orchid-poem.
I only raised
I am not raised orchid-heart.
It's a garden of stones.

돌의 정원-국화 (A garden of stones-chrysanthemum flower)
3×35×35cm
회로기판, 구리철사, 알루미늄 호일 (circuit board, copper wire, aluminum foil)
2023

돌의 정원
- 국화

이사할 때
아파트 현관 앞에 황국이 피었다.
향 참 그윽했다, 햇살에,
겨울이 오고
정자나무는
황국향을 품고
노랑나비를 기다렸다.
잘 기다릴 수 있었다.
겨울 땅속
무싹처럼.

A garden of stones
- chrysanthemum flower

When I move house
Yellow chrysanthemum flower bloomed
In front porch of the apartment.
The scent was so deep.
Winter is coming
The spavilion tree incubated
The scent of the yellow chrysanthemum flower
I waited for the yellow butterfly.
I was able to wait well.
Underground in winter
Like a radish sprout.

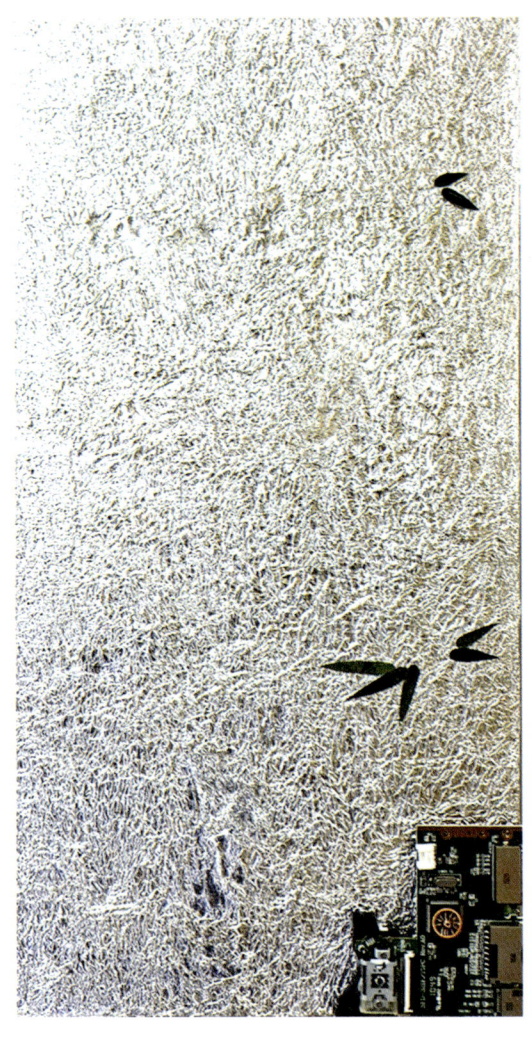

돌의 정원-대나무 (A garden of stones- bamboo)
50×25×1.5cm
회로기판, 알루미늄 호일, 알루미늄 캔 (circuit board, aluminum foil, aluminum can)
2023

돌의 정원
- 대나무

저 돌,
기둥 솟아나리라.
정신의 기둥
내 눈에 보이지 않아도
댓잎 사철 푸르른
까닭이다.

A garden of stones
- bamboo

That stone,

The pillar will rise.

A pillar of the spirit

Even if can't see it with my eyes

Green all year round

That's why.

희망의 힘으로 2 (With the power of hope. 2)
24×80×43cm
구리철사, 회로기판, 매화 가지, 종이, 플라스틱
(copper wire, circuit board, plum branch, paper, plastic)
2022

희망의 힘으로.2

향기는 먼 데서 곁으로 온다.
희망은 보이지 않는 햇살,
향기는 겨울에 가장 환하다.

With the power of hope.2

The scent comes from far away.
Hope is the invisible sunlight,
The scent is brightest in winter.

희망의 힘으로 3 (With the power of hope, 3)
24×67×30cm
구리철사, 회로기판, 플라스틱, 소나무 가지, 모래
(copper wire, circuit board, plastic, pine branches, sand)
2022

희망의 힘으로.3

저 솔잎 푸르러.

With the power of hope.3

Because those pine leaves are green.

희망의 힘으로 8 (With the power of hope. 8)
7×57×70cm
구리철사, 회로기판, 알루미늄 호일 (copper wire, circuit board, aluminum foil)
2022

희망의 힘으로.8

큰 나무는 하루아침에 자라지 않는다.
희망은 오랫동안 보이지 않는다.
기다려라. 보수 없는 노동처럼.
희망은 혁명처럼 화산처럼 폭발한다.

With the power of hope.8

A big tree doesn't grow overnight.

Hope doesn't seem to show up for a long time.

Wait. Like unpaid labor.

Hope explodes like a revolution, like a volcano.

희망의 힘으로 9 (With the power of hope, 9)
8×57×71cm
구리철사, 회로기판, 알루미늄 호일 (copper wire, circuit board, aluminum foil)
2022

희망의 힘으로.9

가로등에 절망이 자랑스러울 때까지.

With the power of hope.9

Until despair is proud on the streetlight.

희망의 힘으로 10 (With the power of hope. 10)
5×59×80cm
구리철사, 회로기판, 자개, 알루미늄 호일
(copper wire, circuit board, mother-of-pearl, aluminum foil)
2022

희망의 힘으로. 10

섬은 가라앉지 않았다.

With the power of hope. 10

The island did not sink.

초롱이탑 2 (Chorong Tower, 2)
22×29.5×49cm
회로기판, 자개, 목재, 구리철사 (circuit board, mother-of-pearl, wood, copper wire)
2023

초롱이탑.2

가로 29.5cm, 세로 22cm, 높이 49cm
죽은 나무
타버린 코일
폐회로기판
버린 자개
죽은 초롱이 깃털.

묻어
뼈마디 소멸이 된들
너와 내가 생성한 마음의 이중나선
영혼의 DNA는
세상의 모든 이별에게
불멸하리라.

Chorong Tower.2

29.5cm wide, 22cm long, and 4cm high
A dead tree
A burnt coilclosed circuit board
A bandoned mother-of-pearl
A dead Chorong feather.

Put it on me
The bones that have been destroyed
The double helix of the heart you and I created
The DNA of the soul is
To all the separation in the world
It will be immortalized.

연리지 (Yeonliji)
80×58×33cm
백자, 사각화분, 회로기판 조각, 나무줄기, 자개 (white porcelain, square flower pot, piece of circuit board, tree trunk, mother-of-pearl)
2023

연리지連理枝

네가 나를 보고
내가 널 보고

하늘이 땅에 닿은 지평선에
강물이 구름에 이른 수평선에
우리가 산다.

이별이 어디 있고
만남이 어디 있으랴.

꿈이 여기고
생이 여기다.

Yeonliji連理枝

When you look at me
I'll look at you

On the horizon where the sky touches the ground
On the horizon where the river reaches the clouds
We live.

There's no such thing as a breakup
There's no way we'll meet.

Dream is here
Life is here.

눈물 위 (Above the tears)
27×29×23cm
구리철사, 회로기판, 화분, 알루미늄 호일, 물, 모래, 수초, 스티로폼 (copper wire, circuit board, flower pot, aluminum foil, water, sand, aquatic plants, styrofoam)
2022

눈물 위	Above the tears

더는 갈 데 없이
웅덩이에 모인 꽃잎.

또 한바탕
모지락스런 빗발에
남은 꽃잎마저
나무에서 쫓겨난다.

먼저 온 꽃잎
나중 온 꽃잎
옹송옹송

구석진 웅덩이에서
얇은 몸 서로 겹쳐
새꽃밭이다.

눈물에 빠지지 않고
눈물 위에서.

With no place to go anymore
Petals collected in a puddle.

Another bout
In the prickly rain
Even the remaining petals
Get kicked out of the tree.

Petals that came first
Petals that came later
Ongsong ongsong

Huddled together
In a cornered puddle
Thin bodies overlap
A new flower garden.

Don't fall into tears
On the tears.

병풍 (Screen)
46×150×160cm
구리철사, 회로기판, 목재, 알루미늄 호일, 자수 (copper wire, circuit board, wood, aluminum foil, embroidery)
2022

병풍

부패 아닌 문명
발효하는 문명
술병이
그대를 기다린다.
길을 펼쳐라.

Screen

Civilization, not corruption

Fermenting civilization

The wine bottle

Wait for you.

Open the road.

소실점에서 (At the vanishing point)
48.5×28.5×6cm
회로기판, 구리철사 (circuit board, copper wire)
2023

소실점에서

영혼이 다하고
몸이 다한 소실점에서
우린 부활한다.
죽음 너머로
인간의 생명을 넘어
우주의 생명으로.

At the vanishing point

With all one's soul

At the point of exhaustion of one's body

We are resurrected.

Beyond death

Beyond human life

To the life of the universe.

박헌영 조형시집
모든 벽은 문이다
ⓒ 박헌영, 2025

발행일	2025년 5월 22일
지은이	박헌영
발행인	이영옥
펴 낸 곳	도서출판 이든북
출판등록	제2001-000003호
주　　소	대전광역시 동구 중앙로 193번길 73
전화번호	(042)222-2536	팩스(042)222-2530
전자우편	eden-book@daum.net
카　페	https://cafe.daum.net/eden-book
공 급 처	한국출판협동조합
	전화 (02)716-5616　(031)944-8234~6

ISBN 979-11-6701-348-4 (03810)
값 17,000원

* 이 책의 판권은 지은이와 이든북에 있습니다.
* 이 책 내용의 전부 또는 일부를 재사용하려면 반드시
  양측에 서면 동의를 받아야 합니다.